0 8 APR 2019
1 4 OCT 2019

1 6 DEC 2019

In order to avoid charges, please return or renew this item by the last date shown.

Online: https://arena.yourlondonlibrary.net/web/ealing

Phone: 0333 370 4700

London Borough of Ealing

Library and Information Services

EALING LIBRARIES www.ealing.gov.uk

Bodies of Water

Lakes

Erika L. Shores

raintree
a Capstone company — publishers for children

Raintree is an imprint of Capstone Global Library Limited, a company incorporated in England and Wales having its registered office at 264 Banbury Road, Oxford, OX2 7DY – Registered company number: 6695582

www.raintree.co.uk
myorders@raintree.co.uk

Text © Capstone Global Library Limited 2019
The moral rights of the proprietor have been asserted.

All rights reserved. No part of this publication may be reproduced in any form or by any means (including photocopying or storing it in any medium by electronic means and whether or not transiently or incidentally to some other use of this publication) without the written permission of the copyright owner, except in accordance with the provisions of the Copyright, Designs and Patents Act 1988 or under the terms of a licence issued by the Copyright Licensing Agency, Barnard's Inn, 86 Fetter Lane, London, EC4A 1EN (www.cla.co.uk). Applications for the copyright owner's written permission should be addressed to the publisher.

Editor: Helen Cox Cannons
Designer: Bobbie Nuytten
Media researcher: Morgan Walters
Production Specialist: Tori Abraham

ISBN 978 1 4747 5838 3
22 21 20 19 18
10 9 8 7 6 5 4 3 2 1

Acknowledgements
Shutterstock: Alberto Loyo, 5, ehrlif, Cover, 1, Eleanor Hennessy, 11, Erni, 19, faber1893, 21, J. Marijs, 17, Proskurina Yuliya, (wave) design element throughout, Ric Schafer, 15, Sergey Ryzhov, 7, Tom Silver, 9, vicspacewalker, 13.

Every effort has been made to contact copyright holders of material reproduced in this book. Any omissions will be rectified in subsequent printings if notice is given to the publisher.

All the internet addresses (URLs) given in this book were valid at the time of going to press. However, due to the dynamic nature of the internet, some addresses may have changed, or sites may have changed or ceased to exist since publication. While the author and publisher regret any inconvenience this may cause readers, no responsibility for any such changes can be accepted by either the author or the publisher.

Printed and bound in India

Contents

What is a lake?. 4

How are lakes made?. 10

What can you find in lakes? . . 16

Glossary 22
Find out more 23
Comprehension questions. . . .24
Index. 24

What is a lake?

A lake is a body of water. Land is all around a lake. There are millions of lakes around the world.

Most lakes hold fresh water. Lake Superior in North America is the largest freshwater lake in the world. Some lakes hold salt water.

Lake water can freeze over when the weather gets very cold. The water under the ice is warmer so it does not freeze.

How are lakes made?

Over thousands of years, glaciers slowly moved rocks. This made holes in the ground.

Glaciers slowly melted over time. The water from the glaciers filled the holes in the ground. This made lakes.

Earthquakes have also made lakes. Many years ago, earthquakes shook the Earth. They made cracks in the ground. Water filled the cracks. It made lakes.

What can you find in lakes?

Plants called bulrushes grow along the sides of lakes. They have long, brown flowers called catkins.

Many fish live in lakes. Roach, trout, carp and pike are some fish that live in freshwater lakes.

People like to swim and play in lakes. They paddle in canoes. People also sail on lakes in boats.

Glossary

bulrush tall, thin plant with long, brown flowers called catkins

earthquake very strong shaking of the ground

freeze become solid at a very low temperature

fresh water water that is not salty

glacier large, slow-moving sheet of ice

Find out more

Lakes (Water, Water Everywhere!), Diyan Leake (Raintree, 2014)

This Drop of Water: A Look at Water Cycles, Anna Claybourne (Franklin Watts, 2018)

Water Sources (Water In Our World), Rebecca Olien (Raintree, 2016)

Websites

You can find out more facts about lakes on the following websites:

kidsgeo.com/geography-for-kids/lakes/

www.natgeokids.com/uk/discover/science/nature/water-cycle/

www.sciencekids.co.nz/sciencefacts/earth/lakes.html

Comprehension questions

1. Describe a glacier. Use the glossary to help you.
2. What can happen to a lake when the temperature gets very cold?
3. Name some fish that are found in lakes.

Index

bulrushes 16
cold 8
cracks 14
earthquakes 14
fish 18
freezing 8
glaciers 10

holes 10, 12
land 4
people 20
plants 16
rocks 10
swimming 18, 20